Count On

5 6 7 8 9 9¢

10 ¢

¢

¢

¢

¢

¢

Count the Money

dime	nickel	penny
10¢	5¢	1¢

 ____ ¢	 ____ ¢	 ____ ¢
 ____ ¢	 ____ ¢	 ____ ¢
 ____ ¢	 ____ ¢	 ____ ¢

How much money do you see?

¢

¢

¢

¢

¢

¢

¢

¢

¢

How much money do I have?

Tom	57¢	Kim	36¢	Nell	29¢
Carlos	53¢	Lester	32¢	Sally	48¢

Put the right name on each coin purse.

Count On

25 ___ 30 ___ 35 ___ 36 ___ 37 ___ 38 ___ 39 ___ 39 ¢

_____ _____ _____ _____ _____ _____ ¢

_____ _____ _____ _____ ¢

_____ _____ _____ _____ _____ _____ ¢

_____ _____ _____ _____ _____ _____ _____ ¢

_____ _____ _____ _____ _____ _____ _____ _____ ¢

_____ _____ _____ _____ _____ _____ ¢

I Love Cookies!

Circle how much money
I need to buy these cookies.

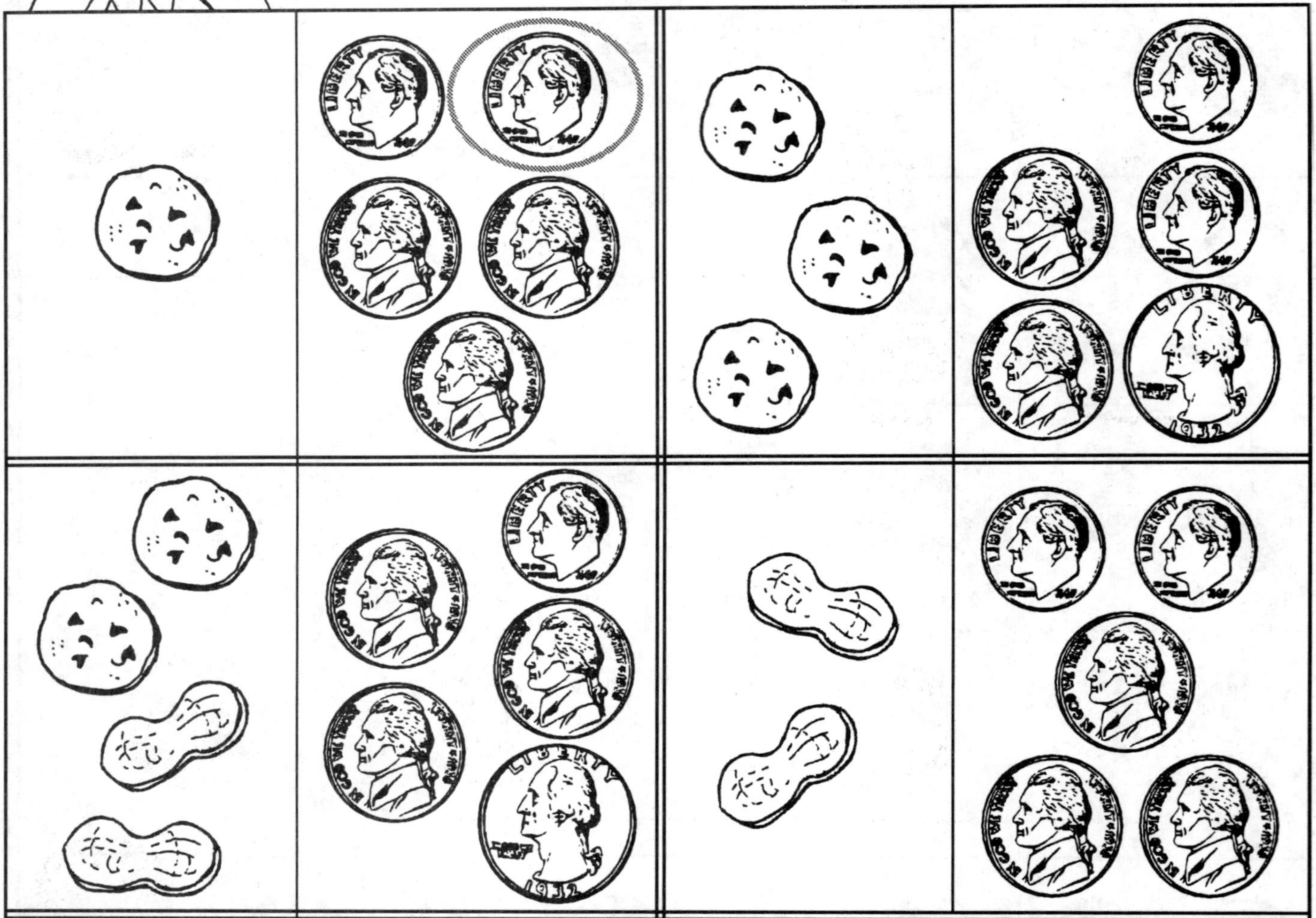

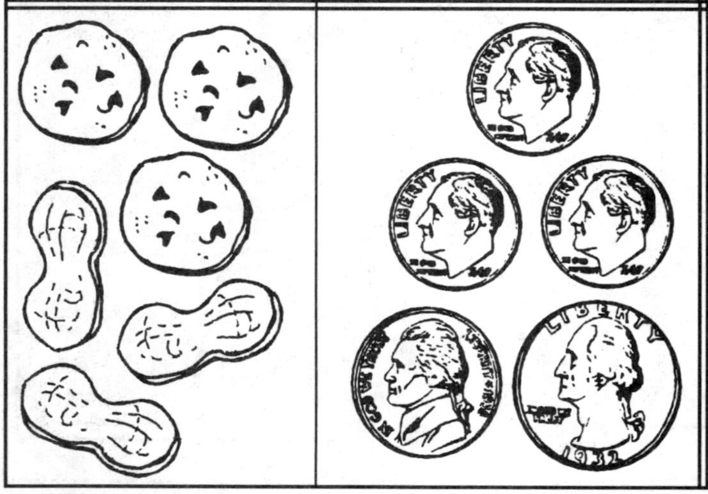

I spent 35¢.
How many cookies did I buy?

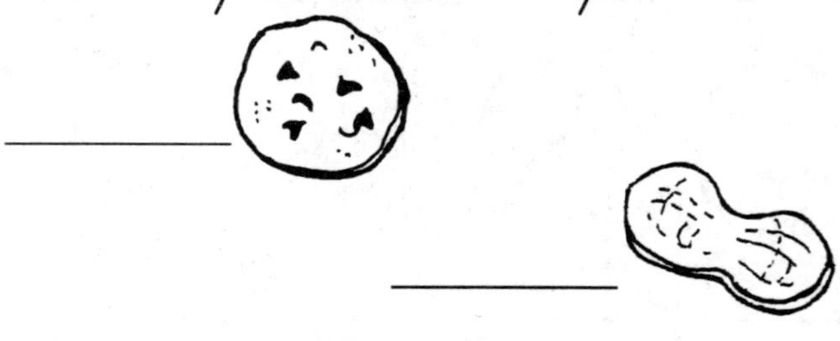

Find the Coins

4 coins = 26¢

3 coins = 35¢

3 coins = 20¢

5 coins = 27¢

3 coins = 21¢

4 coins = 45¢

Circle the coins to make these amounts.

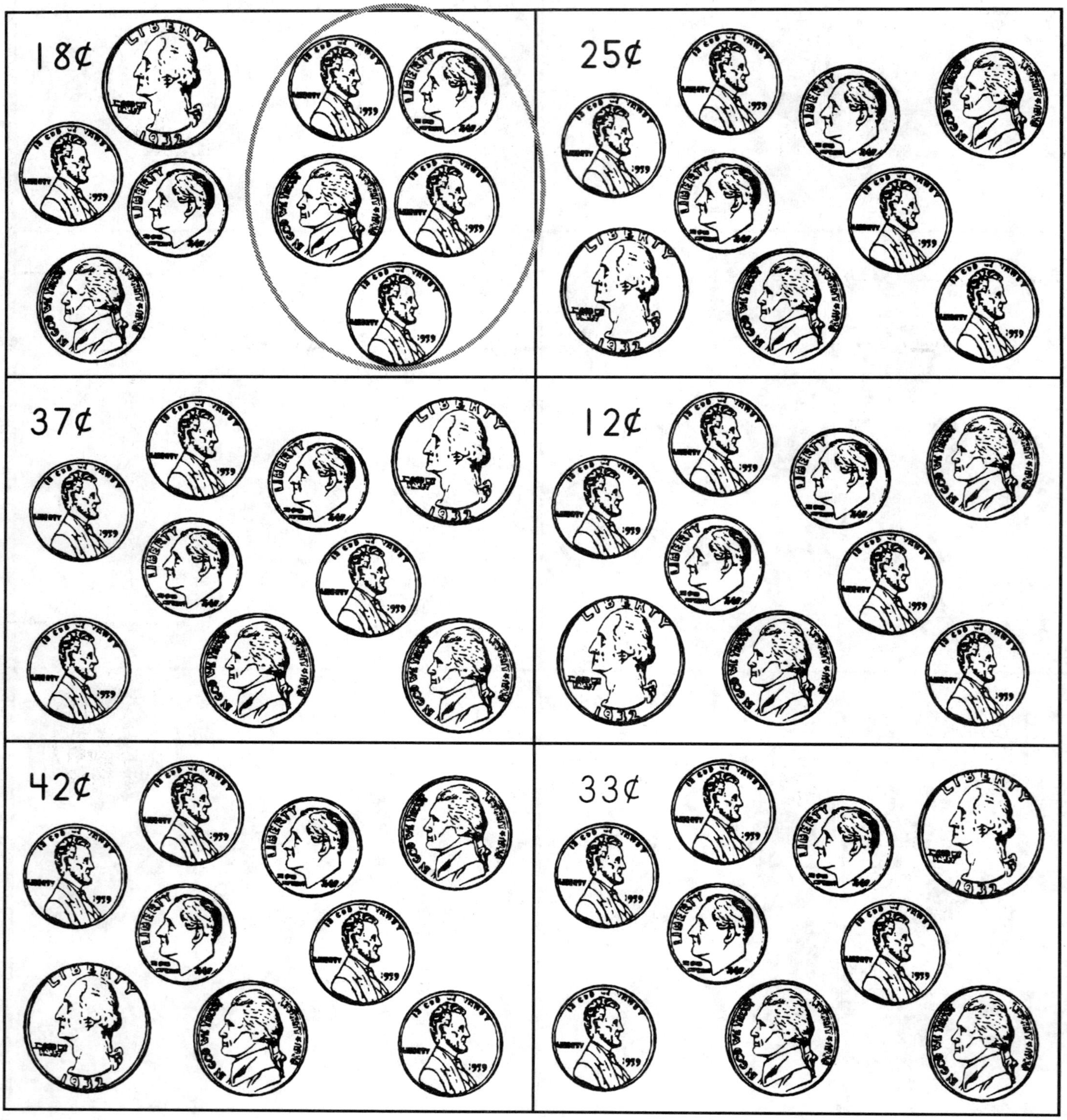

Tic-Tac-Toe

X 25¢ O 50¢

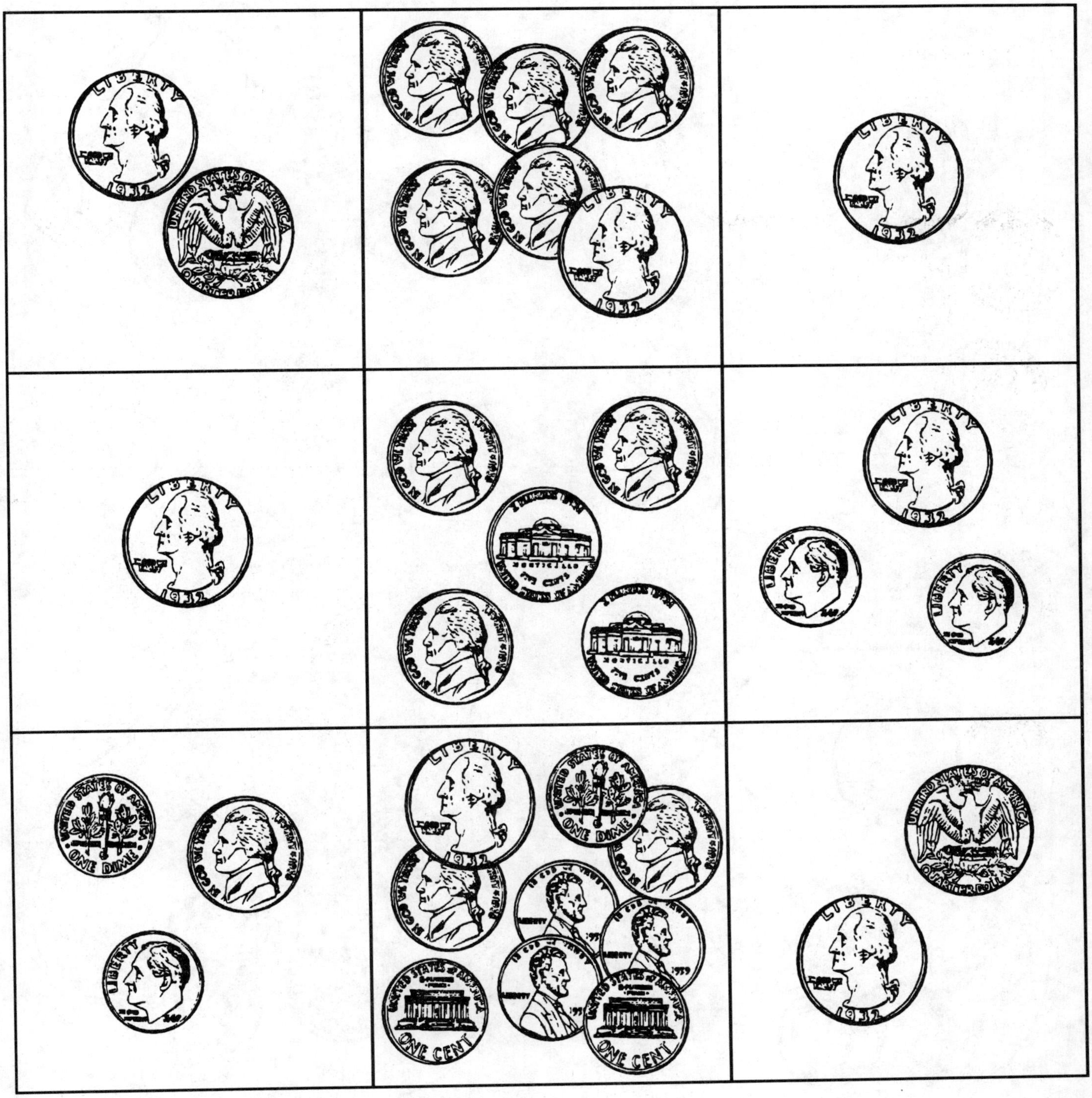

Who won? X or O ____________

How much is in each bank?

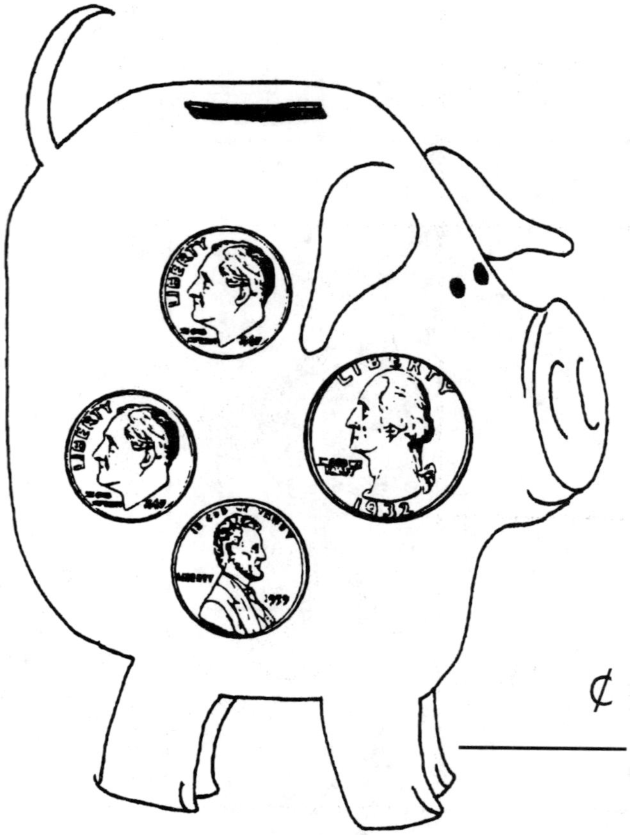

I have:	I get:	How much do I have in all?
32¢		____ ¢
25¢		____ ¢
19¢		____ ¢
80¢		____ ¢
54¢		____ ¢
65¢		____ ¢

Counting Quarters

¢

¢

¢

¢

¢

¢

Greater than	Less than	Equal to
>	<	=

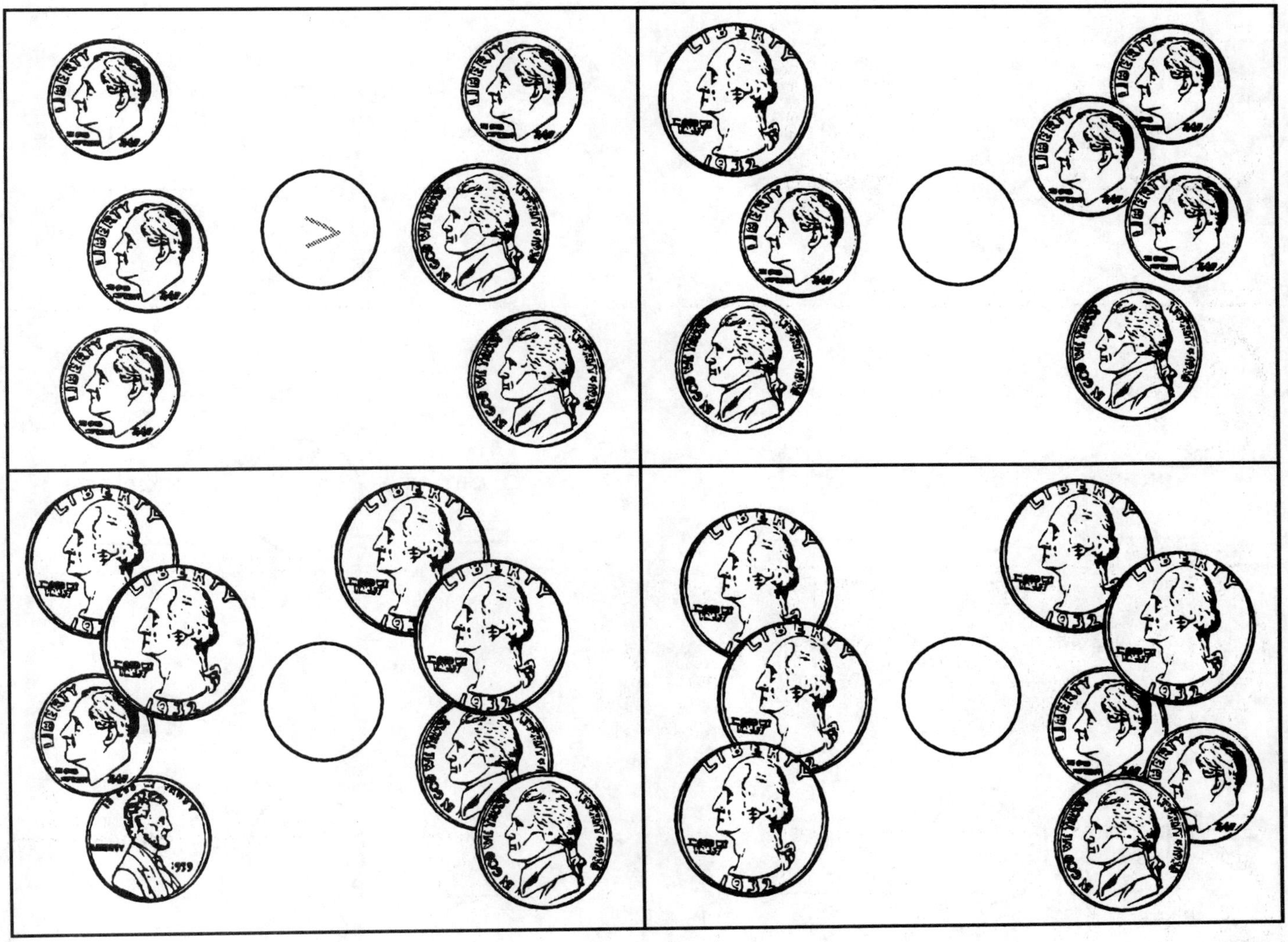

27¢ < 72¢　　57¢ ◯ 97¢　　92¢ ◯ 72¢

36¢ ◯ 41¢　　83¢ ◯ 38¢　　49¢ ◯ 49¢

Greater than Less than Equal to

(>) (<) (=)

How much is it?
Which is the most?

3 nickels 15 ¢	<	2 dimes 20 ¢
5 nickels ____ ¢	◯	1 quarter ____ ¢
1 quarter ____ ¢	◯	4 nickels ____ ¢
5 dimes ____ ¢	◯	2 quarters ____ ¢
15 pennies ____ ¢	◯	5 nickels ____ ¢
9 dimes ____ ¢	◯	7 dimes ____ ¢
1 quarter ____ ¢	◯	3 dimes ____ ¢
30 pennies ____ ¢	◯	4 nickels ____ ¢

half dollar 50 cents $.50

Color sets of 50 cents red.
Color sets of 25 cents blue.
Color sets of 5 cents yellow.

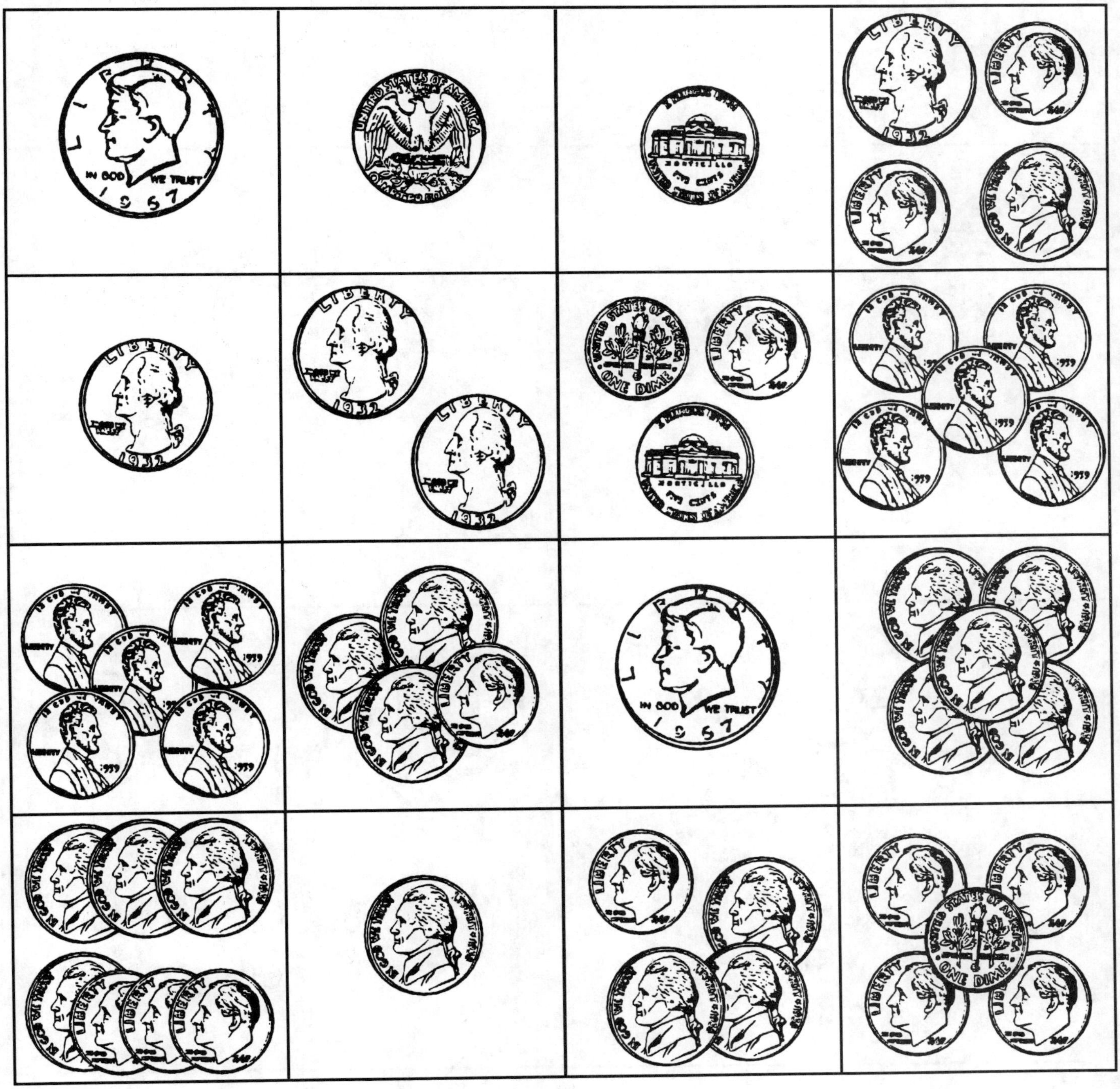

Circle the Amount

a. 90¢
b. 63¢
c. 38¢

a. 60¢
b. 30¢
c. 51¢

a. 55¢
b. 37¢
c. 10¢

a. 80¢
b. 53¢
c. 71¢

a. 65¢
b. 25¢
c. 29¢

a. 80¢
b. 76¢
c. 55¢

Match the coins to the amount.

a.

30¢

e.

60¢

b.

27¢

f.

50¢

c.

65¢

g.

75¢

d.

35¢

h.

43¢

Count to $1.00

1.  $ .50 $ 1.00

2.  $ __.__ $ __.__ $ __.__ $ __.__

3.  $ __.__ $ __.__ $ __.__ $ __.__ $ __.__
$ __.__ $ __.__ $ __.__ $ __.__ $ __.__

4.  $ __.__ $ __.__ $ __.__ $ __.__ $ __.__
$ __.__ $ __.__ $ __.__ $ __.__ $ __.__
$ __.__ $ __.__ $ __.__ $ __.__ $ __.__
$ __.__ $ __.__ $ __.__ $ __.__ $ __.__

5. How many  in $1.00? __________

How many  in $1.00? __________

How many  in $1.00? __________

How many  in $1.00? __________

How many  in $1.00? __________

Match the coins to the amount.

a.

52¢

40¢

e.

b.

63¢

21¢

f.

c.

42¢

76¢

g.

d.

50¢

67¢

h.

Circle coins to make sets of $1.00.

How many sets of $1.00 did you find?

Making Change

Costs:	You have:	Left:
 32¢		____ ¢
 89¢		____ ¢
 53¢		____ ¢
 71¢		____ ¢
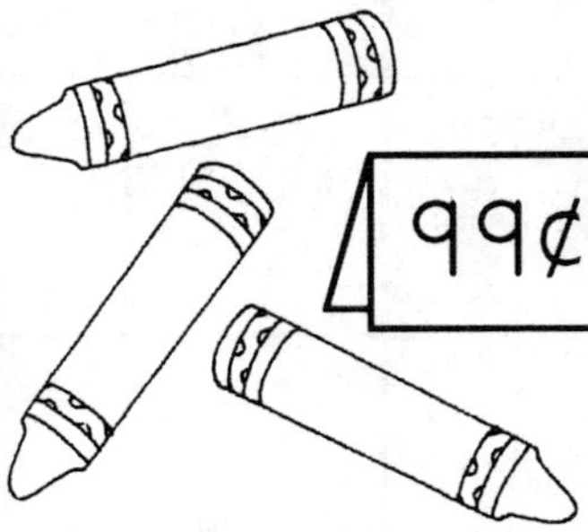 99¢		____ ¢

How many coins do you need?

	 10	 5	 1
9¢		1	4
11¢			
16¢			
24¢			

	 50	 25	 10	 5	 1
56¢	1			1	1
75¢					
48¢					
39¢					

Circle coins to make sets of $1.00.

Dollar Sign $ Decimal Point .

Put the dollar sign and decimal point where they belong.

187 = $1.87 ______   210 = ______

479 = ______   107 = ______

333 = ______   598 = ______

Count the money

$ 1.20

$ ___ . ___

$ ___ . ___

$ ___ . ___

$ ___ . ___

$ ___ . ___

Match the bills.

How much money do you see?

$ 5.75

$ ___ . ___

$ ___ . ___

$ ___ . ___

$ ___ . ___

$ ___ . ___

Helping Grandpa

Maggie helped her grandpa clean out his garage. He told her she could have any of the cans, soda bottles, glass, or newspapers she found. Maggie was delighted. When she sold what she had cleaned out of the garage, she had made a lot of money.

1. Maggie found 18 aluminum cans and 24 soda bottles. She got 3 cents for each of the cans and 10 cents for each bottle. How much money did she get?

   $ ____.______

2. She sold the newspapers by the pound. She got 12 cents for each of the 20 pounds of newspapers she carried away. How much did she get for the newspapers?

   $ ____.______

3. Finally, she sold a box of old glass jars. She got 7 cents a pound for the glass. She was surprised to find that the box of glass weighed 48 pounds. How much money did she get for the glass?

   $ ____.______

4. What was the total amount of money Maggie got for the bottles, cans, glass, and newspapers?

   $ ____.______

How much does your name cost?

vowels	"tail" letters	all other letters
$.50	$1.00	$.25
a e i o u	g j p q y	

Sam	Leroy	Reggy
$ .25 .50 .25 $.		
My first name	My middle name	My last name

Sums and Differences

$ 2.50

\+ 1.32

$.

$

\+

$.

$ 6.60

− 1.35

$.

$ 16.53

− 5.28

$.

$ 4.95	$ 8.31	$ 3.62	$ 8.64	$ 6.21
− 2.49	− 5.74	+ 6.59	+ 2.53	− 5.89
$ 2.46	$.	$.	$.	$.

Making Change

You have:	Cost:	Give clerk:	Change:
	$ .90	$ 1.00	$ .10
	$ 1.30	$.	$.
	$ 1.50	$.	$.
	$ 2.28	$.	$.
	$ 5.08	$.	$.

Answer Key

Please take time to go over the work your child has completed. Ask your child to explain what he/she has done. Praise both success and effort. If mistakes have been made, explain what the answer should have been and how to find it. Let your child know that mistakes are a part of learning. The time you spend with your child helps let him/her know you feel learning is important.

page 1

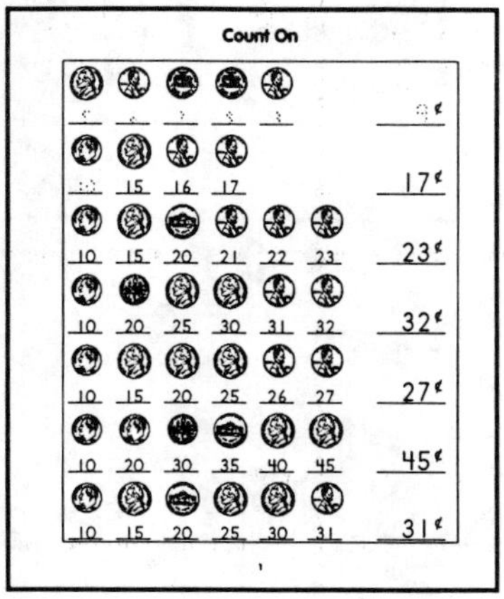

page 2

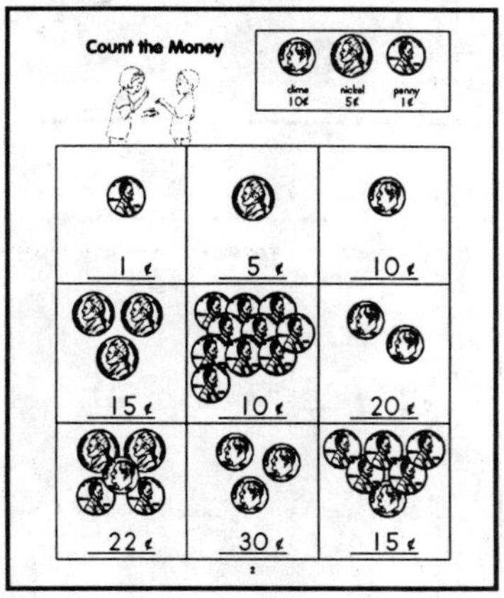

page 3

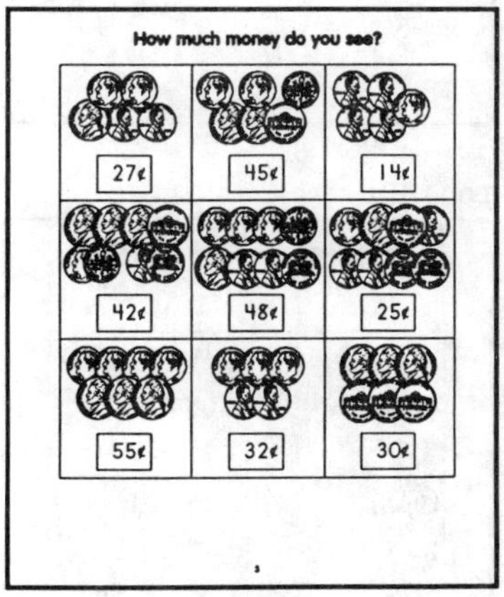

page 4

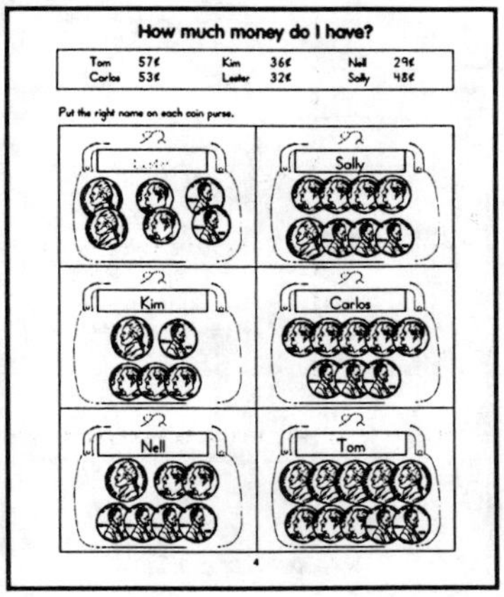

page 5

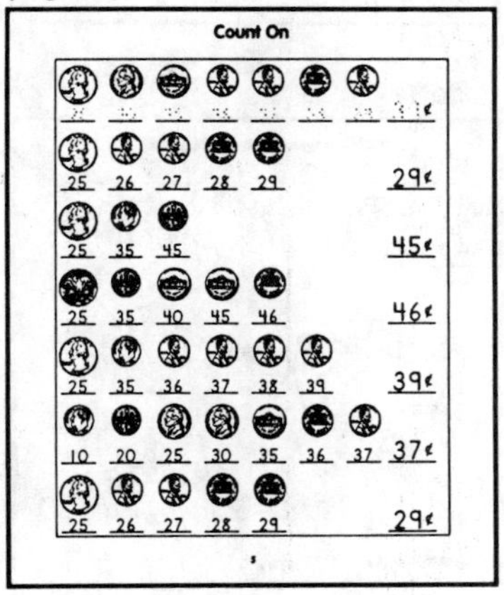

page 6 answers may vary

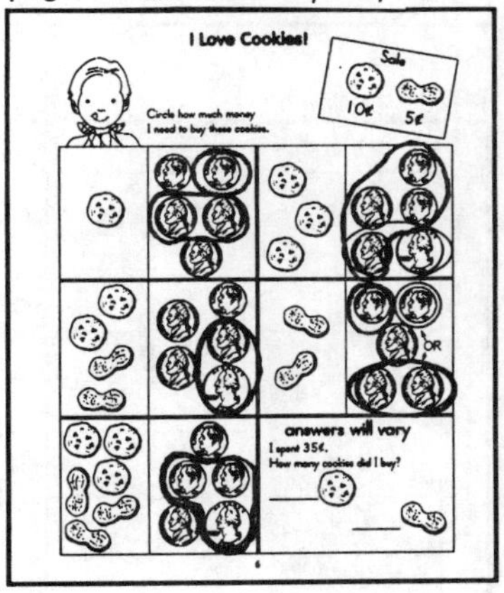

page 7

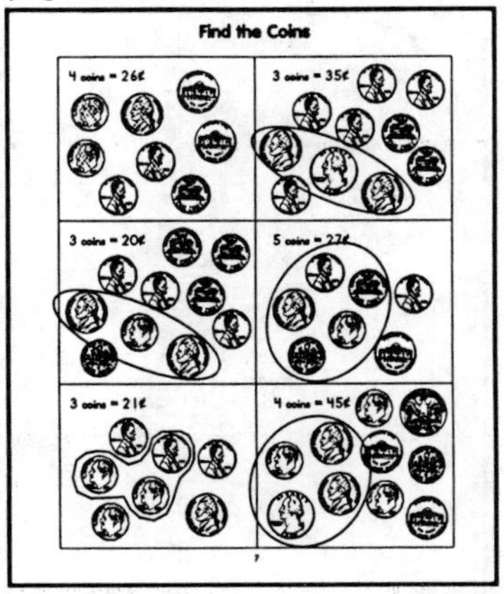

page 8

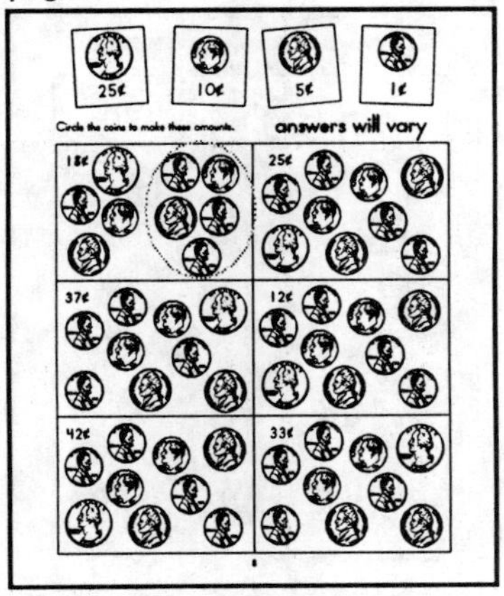

page 9

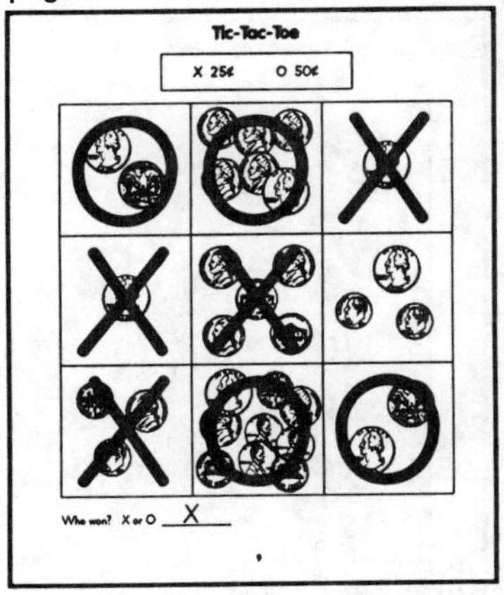

page 10

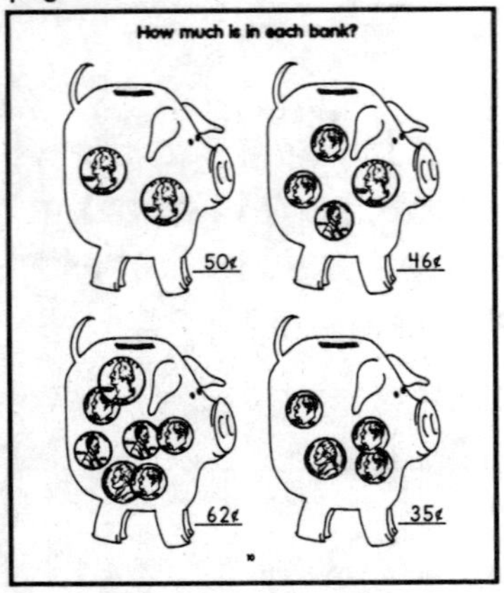

page 11

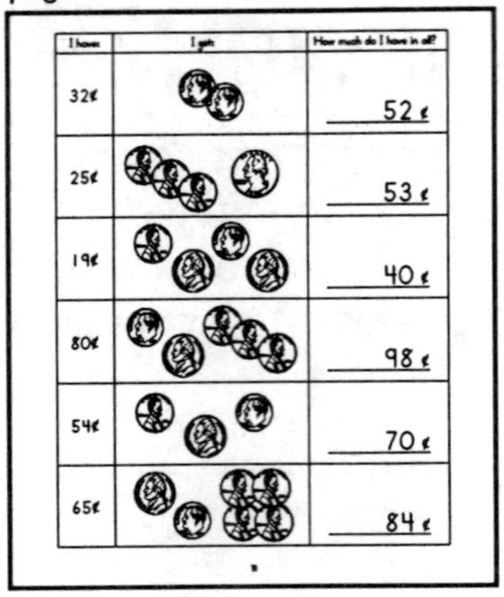

page 12

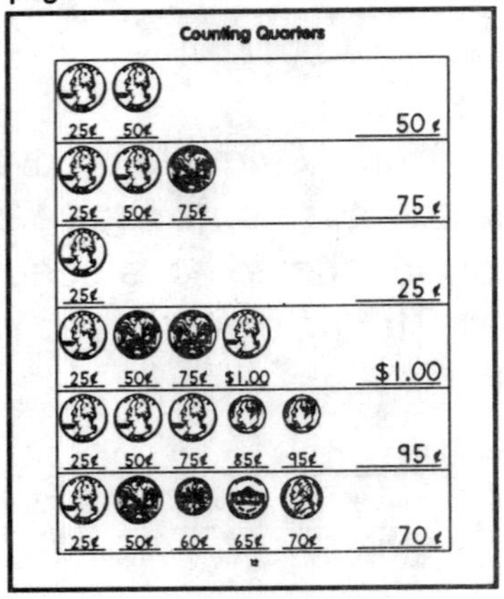

page 13

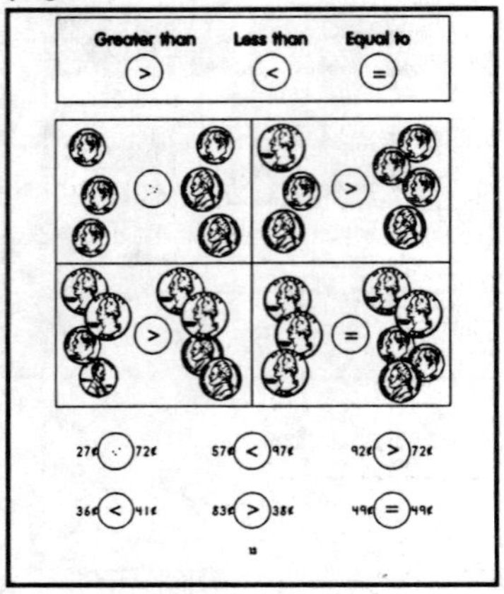

page 14

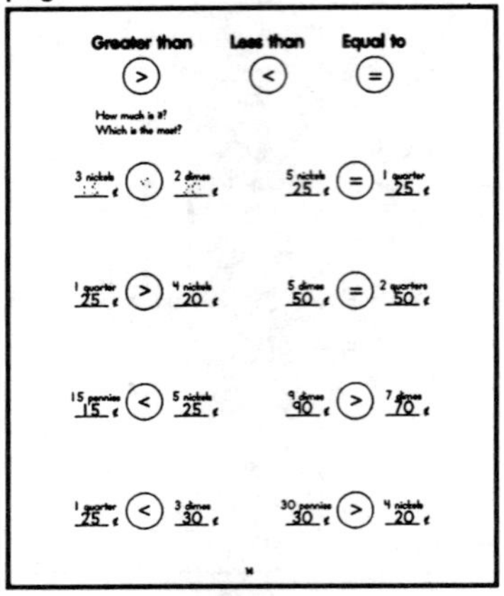

page 15

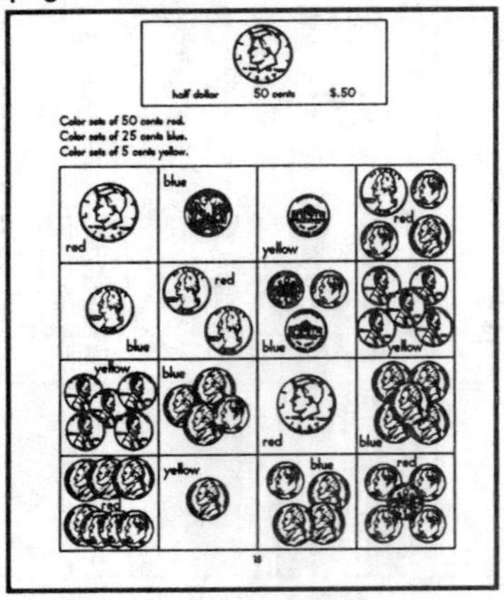

page 16

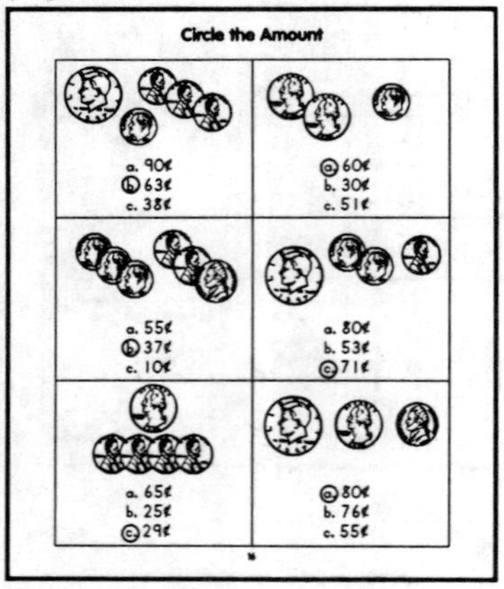

page 17

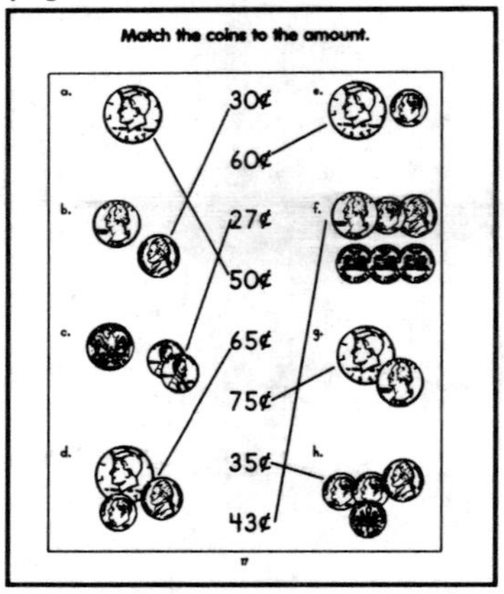

page 18

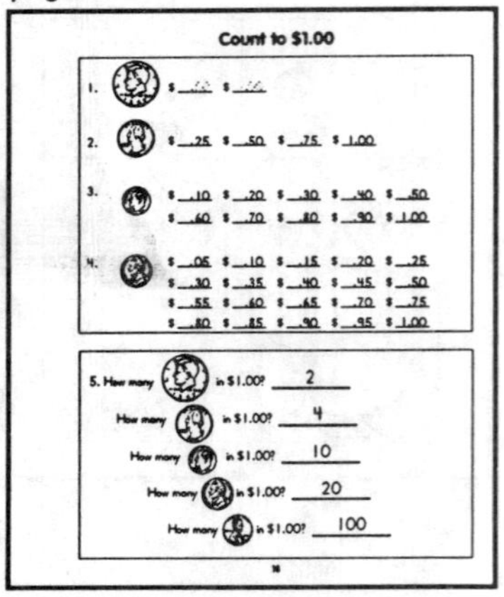

page 19

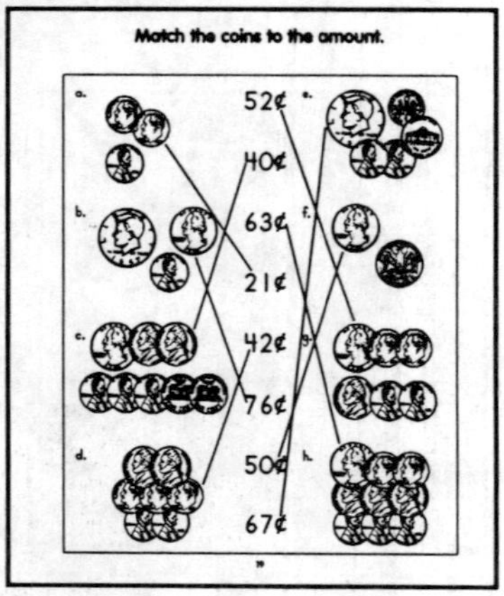

page 20

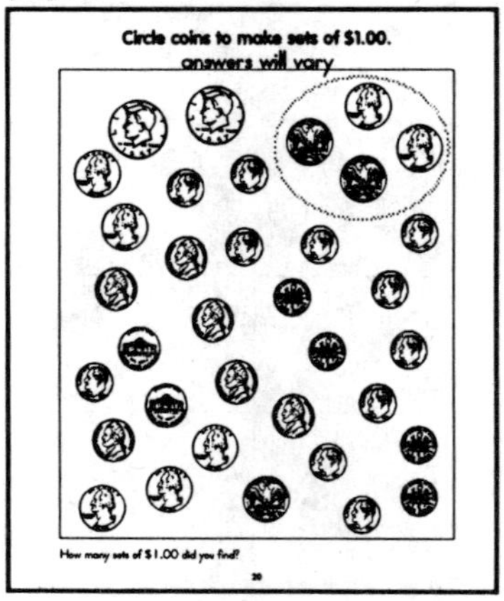

page 21

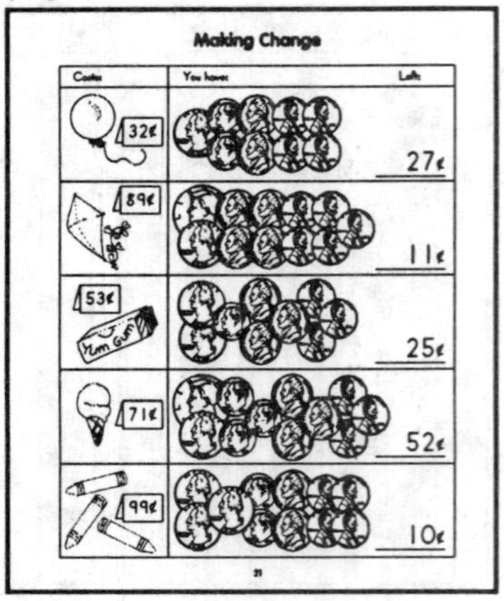